Is it
all over?

**Can football
survive the
Premier
League?**

John Williams

SOUTH
Street
PRESS

Is it all over?
Can football survive the Premier League?

South Street Press is an imprint of
Garnet Publishing Limited

Published by
Garnet Publishing Limited
8 Southern Court
South Street
Reading
RG1 4QS
UK

ISBN 1 902932 01 3

First Edition 1999

British Library Cataloguing-in-Publication
Data. A catalogue record for this book is
available from the British Library.

House editor: Natalie Hutchin
Jacket and book design: Michael Hinks
Printed in Lebanon

Contents

Introduction

This book examines the origins and the extraordinary commercial success of the FA Premier League and also its effects on English football in a wider sense. It also considers the effects of the new League and changes in the sport in an international context. From 1992, when the new League was first established, the professional game in England at the very highest levels has enjoyed an economic and cultural boom of quite unprecedented proportions in the postwar period. The new League has been the catalyst for a tremendous growth in popular interest in top English football, after a long period when public discussion about the sport focused largely on concerns about its associated and highly publicised problems of hooliganism and crowd control. It might have been expected, then, that this new era in the development of the sport would have been wholeheartedly embraced in England by both commentators and avid football supporters as something of a 'golden age' in the game's history. Instead, opinions on the effects and longer-term consequences of the formation of the FA Premier League vary wildly.

The Changing Face
of Football Culture

There is rather more agreement on the growing cultural importance of sport, especially football, in post-industrial societies. Writing recently in the *Observer* (13 July 1997), the cultural critic Martin Jacques described the 1990s as the 'Age of Sport'. Just as rock music became the dominant cultural form in the 1960s and 1970s and possibly, briefly and less forcefully, comedy the key form in the 1980s, so it is now sport, especially football, which is apparently ubiquitous, the metaphor of the time. According to this view, Nike and even Manchester United are, as much as Coca-Cola, the commercial 'brands' of the age. Every British broadsheet newspaper now tries to promote extra sales with a distinctive football-dominated sports section, and sports magazines and men's magazines with sports copy are numerous and booming in Britain. Football personalities – Zidane, Beckham, Ronaldo, Owen – have become cultural and commercial icons, sought after by sponsors and advertisers alike. Where football was once distinctly lowbrow – of the working people – now it is the stuff of serious literature and of furious debate among the chattering classes. Once, local rich men invested in sport for sentiment rather than for financial gain; now major City institutions and media conglomerates are queuing up to make investments in the 'people's game'.

Jacques goes on to argue that the boom in sport
and in its cultural centrality is connected to the changing
physical and mental rhythms of late-modern life, particularly
to the associated rise in concern with 'the body' in leisure
time. But he also thinks that the rise in sports spectatorship
in Britain is strongly linked to the perceived meritocracy of
late-modern sport in contrast to its Victorian forebears –
more women now watch, for example – and also to the
crucial role of television in disseminating, transforming and
globalising sporting practice, especially sports fandom, for
a swelling international armchair audience.

The 1998 World Cup in France, for example,
attracted an estimated cumulative TV audience of 37 billion
viewers worldwide – twice that of the 1996 Olympic
Games. The worldwide TV audience for the Final was
around 1.7 billion. The Official World Cup Web site also
dealt with a record 38 million hits on just one day during
the Finals. Television rights for the 1998 World Cup Finals
were sold for £54 million (the rights for the 2002 Finals in
Japan and South Korea have been sold, for the first time,
to a European cable TV consortium, Kirch, for some £650
million) to this figure can be added the £236 million in
income (tickets, marketing) from actually staging matches
in France and the estimated £750 million worth of
merchandise sales generated by the Finals. With 30,000
Brazilians alone staying in France for an average of 16
nights during the Finals, the returns, simply from tourism for
the event, were also immense.

Perhaps these are among the reasons why the
Labour Party in Britain seems to be putting so much
political store on this country attracting the World Cup
Finals in 2006 – even though England originally agreed to
back Germany's bid for the event, and the governing body
of world football, FIFA, has made clear its own preference

that the 2006 Finals should go to Africa for the first time. The success of the FA Premier League and the successful staging of Euro '96 has made a World Cup bid by England feasible. Bringing the World Cup to the nation is clearly seen as a major stimulus to domestic business, a real lift to our international standing in the world and a means to promoting a sense of national 'well-being' in the host country. It can also deflect attention from difficult economic and political problems. No wonder, then, that with these sorts of issues and huge financial sums at stake, the public competition for staging mega international sports events is now attracting considerable international public scrutiny because of fears about behind-the-scenes 'political' dealings and the likelihood of corruption.

Notwithstanding these international developments, it is particularly *English* football which seems a central focus for at least some of the wider cultural and commercial shifts identified by several cultural commentators. The current Carling FA Premier League Web site, for example, is reportedly the most popular of its kind in the world. The English game is also widely perceived abroad to have 'solved' its hooligan crisis of the 1970s and 1980s (although there is less certainty about this in England itself) and to have metamorphosed into a mature and dynamic sport which is a commercially successful, cutting edge sports model for the 1990s and the new millennium. Recent figures have shown that top football clubs in England have now overtaken many of their European and world rivals in terms of their marketing effort, and administrators from leagues all around the world now visit the FA Premier League in order to try to discover the 'secret' of the transformation of English football from an historically significant but recently cultish and troubled sport of the 1980s to a major success story less than a decade later.

Football marketing

So, what is new, if anything, about the present period of football's expansion? If, as Jacques argues, the origins of modern sport are the largely masculine articulation of ideals around notions of warfare, territory and national values, then the new, TV-promoted worlds of sport and the patterns of consumption that they generate and shape are arguably increasingly less gendered now, and they also promise to *transcend* ethnic and national boundaries. Today, it is difficult to identify a top club side in England which contains no foreign players. Even the lineage of international footballers is by no means easy to follow these days, and regularly we see players who have a forgotten or obscure relative with some link to a country representing that country internationally. Football, in some accounts, is even fast challenging material objects – factories, plant, machinery – as a measure of 'value' in late-modern societies. What most people in Britain 'know' about Croatia, for example, is pretty much covered by their involvement in recent 'ethnic' wars and their Euro' 96 and 1998 World Cup football triumphs.

On the specific issue of a gender shift in English football, females are regularly identified these days as the largest growth area for English football crowds and for their general growing involvement in the institution of British

The 1997 FA Premier League National Fan Survey (over 28,000 fans) revealed that around 12 per cent of all FA Premier League fans were female. However, it was also shown that around one third of all new fans who had starting attending Premier League matches in the previous five years were female.

football as players, journalists and administrators. Although the number of women who work at executive levels in FA Premier League clubs is still very small, their presence is slowly growing. There are certainly more women football presenters on radio and on both terrestrial and satellite TV, even though their appearance on screen sometimes suggests their presence is aimed specifically at a young, male audience. Perhaps when we see older females on sports TV – and as pundits or experts on football, as well as young female presenters, we can be a little more confident about the nature and motives for some of the changes which are certainly occurring here.

In the same way, the complex ideas associated with notions of attracting the 'family' audience to football, an important area for most football marketing in Britain, need careful examination. Is the intention really to target female fans from any background? Or is the real aim to attract specific kinds of people to FA Premier League football – the reasonably affluent and 'well-behaved'; families with children who will want and be able to purchase merchandise; predominantly the young, perhaps. Unpacking what clubs and administrators mean by 'football families' tells us much more about how they would prefer to see football in this country developing over the next decades.

Sporting 'brands' are also among the new international currencies and metaphors of trade these days; for example, every major football club in England, as well as the FA Premier League itself, currently and assiduously attempt to 'plug into' global markets and to improve the value of their distinctive and powerful 'brands'. For instance, in 1997 Manchester United, probably the world's most widely supported club, appointed the investment banking arm of HSBC Midland Bank, which has a dominant position in the money markets in the Far East, to help the club capitalise on research which showed United to be the European football 'brand' most recognised by an Asian audience. Showing an acute awareness of the scope of football 'brand' markets these days, United has recently launched its own branded ketchup and mineral water. Other English football clubs are some way behind United's lead, but Tottenham Hotspur, for example, has also been attempting to purchase football clubs in the Far East in order to help worldwide promotion of the Spurs 'brand'. Targeting another market, Newcastle United has looked to introduce football products sporting the exclusive NUFC 'brand' in the United States. One smaller English club, Crystal Palace, has recently signed two Chinese 'players', at least in part as a way of exploring possible TV and merchandising deals in the People's Republic of China. Clearly, signing foreign footballers these days is not just about trying to improve the team.

Almost at the same time as this global expansion in football markets for top English clubs has been taking place, the exploitative underpinnings of the new global divisions of labour, which sustain the manufacturing domestic and export boom in English football, have been exposed. A Christian Aid report, *Stitching Footballs*, recently confirmed that 30,000 Indian children work in the sports goods industry, producing goods for sale by top British football clubs. Also, the *Wall Street Journal* recently reported that some international football products are being manufactured by forced labour workers in China. The huge profits of international sports goods manufacturers are substantially based on low labour and low material costs in so-called 'third world' economies, where in return they offer employment and modest welfare programmes.

The material costs (in terms of cloth, transport and labour, etc.) of producing a Premier League replica football shirt – which sells for around £40 in England – is estimated to be under £5.

Top Premier League clubs also charge so much now for deals with manufacturers – up to £60 million for a recent shirt deal with Manchester United, for example – that even with sales of hundreds of thousands of shirts, it is usually the clubs, rather than the manufacturers, who now make the really big money here. Of course, the major sports goods companies – such as Umbro, Nike, Reebok and Adidas – make plenty more from their associations with the top football clubs and from their other club products on offer. By the late 1990s football kit accounted for around 11.5 per cent, or £195 million, of all sport and leisure clothing sales in the UK.

Sports clothing sales, £m 1997

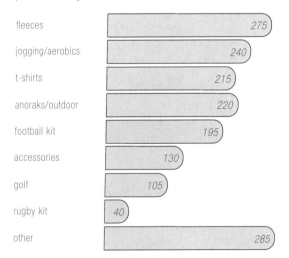

fleeces	275
jogging/aerobics	240
t-shirts	215
anoraks/outdoor	220
football kit	195
accessories	130
golf	105
rugby kit	40
other	285

Total=£1.7bn
Source: Verdict Research, 1998

Players and sponsors

In these new global economies, where brands transcend national boundaries, sporting heroes are also increasingly promoted and experienced as the new role models for the young in late-modern societies where authority and respect no longer relate to some established and ethnically exclusive scale of hierarchy. The 'ironic' street 'blackness' of sports stars such as Ian Wright, Michael Jordan, Tiger Woods and Les Ferdinand is clearly central, for example, to Nike's own global sports sales strategy as well as to more localised sales and product placement. Indeed, the self-consciously inner-city 'ragga' persona of England's Ian Wright is now frequently set against the 'straight' Anglo and timeless sporting hero image of England captain Alan Shearer, at least in terms of their commercial 'branding'. Wright has been seen on British TV advertising Nike and also mobile phones. By contrast, Lucozade, taking advantage of its traditional nature, catapults Shearer back to a 1950s north of England setting, where he is 'coached' in a council house back garden by an old white mentor who instructs him to strike a beaten football against a dusty carpet, hung out to be cleaned. This is certainly a 'place' which pre-dates both the new football technocrats and any talk or popular experience of 'black Britain'. These images of Wright and Shearer bring head to head a 'new' and a much 'older' version of England in the ultimate late-modern language of commercial advertising – and set around the very 'hot' cultural product of the 1990s, namely professional football.

As the Brazilian footballer Ronaldo's recent transfer saga and World Cup drama also demonstrates, advertisers and sports sponsors are now key figures in football at home and abroad. Major sports manufacturers now regard themselves as key actors in the crucial matter of 'placing' their sporting clients for their maximum international sales potential. Nike were rumoured to be seeking a series of loan deals for 'their' player Ronaldo prior to his recent club move to Inter Milan – presumably so they could shunt this footballing human billboard around the lucrative European sports markets. Nike's role in Ronaldo's less-than-complete recovery from illness and his disastrous appearance in the World Cup Final in France 1998 is still unclear. (As is the role of the England football team's sponsors, the Nationwide Building Society, in the departure of England boss, Glenn Hoddle, despite the allegations in some sections of the British press.) What is clear, however, is that any sponsor spending large amounts of cash in support of top stars or teams now expects them to perform 'appropriately' on the largest international sporting stages.

More clear-cut is Nike's role in shaping the future of the Brazilian national team, world football's most powerful and valuable brand. As part of a $170 million, ten-year sponsorship deal with Brazil, Nike is reportedly able to shape that country's international fixture list and to organise 'Nike tours' for the most famous and valuable footballers in the world. A recent Adidas TV advert brought together many of the company's top international football clients to 'play' together in a virtual 'world team' in praise of Adidas Predator boots. It is not too fanciful to imagine at some point in the future, a real Nike v. Adidas match played for huge commercial exposure – and probably shown on cable or satellite TV.

The Origins of the
FA Premier League

Throughout the 1980s the top football clubs in England had sought ways to extricate themselves from their cross-subsidising economic relationships with smaller clubs in the Football League. These arrangements, for transferring money from bigger clubs to smaller ones, were a useful way of regulating competition between those clubs with large followings and those with a much smaller fan base. In the early 1980s all this began to change. Arrangements for sharing the income from matches between the home and the away club were finally ended. This created difficulties for clubs like Wimbledon who then had to pretty much survive on their own home crowds, which were less than one-quarter of the size of some of those elsewhere. Top clubs could now keep all of their gate returns and pull away from others in the Football League.

But this was not enough. In the late 1980s, chairmen from the top English football clubs were caught in secret negotiations over a separate TV deal. It seemed only a matter of time before radical structural change would occur in football – either in the shape of a breakaway of the top clubs, or in terms of a dramatic shake-up in the way money coming into the sport was raised and distributed between clubs. The issue of TV money was especially important here – the lack of real competition for live sports coverage between the BBC and ITV, and the poor public image of football, had kept the value of football TV deals very low in the 1970s and 1980s. They could be measured in just tens of £millions only, and even this cash was relatively evenly and thinly spread among the four divisions of the Football League. The top clubs wanted more TV money to match the football deals being done elsewhere – in France, for example – and they also wanted to keep much more of the total TV kitty raised for themselves. After all, they argued, who exactly did the TV fans want to watch on TV if it wasn't the large and famous clubs?

While this debate was simmering, something happened which was to help accelerate and give shape to changes which already seemed likely to shift the whole course of English football in the final decade of the twentieth century. On 15 April 1989, 96 Liverpool supporters died in a terrible stadium disaster at Hillsborough. The official inquiry report on the disaster, the Taylor Report, blamed the disaster on operational mistakes made on the day by the police. The disaster was clearly connected to the lack of generally civilised provisions for supporters and to the, then, prevailing anxieties about hooliganism which helped to convert many English football stadia effectively into a collection of embattled – and ultimately deadly – pens. But the author of the report, Lord Justice Taylor, also argued that the events at Hillsborough symbolised wider failings in the game, including a lack of effective leadership in English football – a sport which had seemed to be simply lurching from crisis to crisis since the late 1960s.

A power struggle for control of English football then ensued. How could the top clubs 'use' the uncertain aftermath of Hillsborough to make their escape from the clutches of the old Football League? When help arrived, it came from an unexpected source. The Football

The Taylor Report (1990)

This is arguably the most important and far-reaching official inquiry into a domestic football tragedy and also something of a 'visionary' document in terms of mapping out important aspects of a new future for the sport. Taylor, for the first time in a case of this kind, allowed football fans official representation at his inquiry and did not limit his own remarks or recommendations to the incidents at Hillsborough alone. Instead, he commented on the cultural significance of football, the poor leadership within the sport – which, he argued, had taken too little notice of previous disasters – and the relative lack of involvement of football supporters in the decision-making processes of football. He even recommended against a new piece of proposed legislation by the Thatcher government for the introduction of 'membership' (identity) cards for football fans.

Taylor helped revolutionise safety procedures at stadia, which meant new stadium safety officers and stewards, with training to match, and a greatly reduced role for the police in the management of football fans. Today, it is a statutory requirement that appropriate medical support is on stand-by at football stadia in case of a tragedy occurring.

However, Taylor will probably be best remembered for his insistence that modern football stadia needed to be all-seated to guard against similar tragedies occurring again. His enforced deadlines and steadfastness on this point may not have been welcomed by all football fans, many of whom continued to want to stand, but without this approach it is hard to imagine the development of the new generation of football grounds we have seen since 1990. With seats, for example, came the dismantling of perimeter fencing – a change welcomed by all fans. Taylor envisaged all-seated stadia operating at the sorts of ticket prices which would allow access for all supporters. Instead, in the 1990s the game began to market itself successfully to a new sort of fan and ticket prices soared as facilities improved and 'exotic' new foreign stars were attracted into the FA Premier League.

Association (FA), usually seen as the patrician arm of the amateur traditions of the sport in England, was increasingly a body becoming alerted to the commercial ways in which the sport was being transformed internationally. The FA controlled the England national team and so had a direct interest in establishing stronger links with the top clubs, from which most international players were drawn. In 1991, the FA published its revolutionary *Blueprint for Football*, which set out plans not only for an overhaul of coaching, football stadia and refereeing in England, but also for the establishment of an entirely new league: the FA Premier League. The FA involvement enabled top clubs to claim that the new league was not about greed, but rather was needed for the general good of the English game and to help the national team.

The central marketing and social premises for the launch of a new TV-funded FA Premier League in the more optimistic post-Hillsborough climate of early 1990s English football were based on predictions of likely increasing social and economic divisions in Britain. Calls for more unified and more assertive forms of leadership in the sport in the 'liberal' Taylor Report into the Hillsborough tragedy produced this opportunist move by the game's governing body, the Football Association. In tandem with senior Football League clubs who were seeking to dissolve financial ties with struggling clubs in the lower reaches of the 103-year-old, 92-club Football League, the FA established a new and distinctive 'blue chip' league format. The result was the first football league in England to be funded by, and substantially for, television.

An analysis of social and leisure trends for the 1990s produced for the FA *Blueprint* by the private leisure consultancy, the Henley Centre for Forecasting, noted the 'dramatic affluence gains' of the 1980s in Britain and the growing disparity between rich and poor during that decade, as well as the 'increasing division between public sector and private sector facilities . . . developments rooted in reactions to fundamental class, affluence and attitude shifts' (p. 8). In this account, football is a mass spectator sport which carries social and psychological baggage from a very different era of social stratification and leisure pursuits to those promised for Britain in the 1990s. The analysts' conclusions were quite explicit:

> In the 1990s and beyond, patterns of affluence and the associated fragmentation of circumstances and interests may make it almost impossible to formulate any leisure activity as a truly mass market one. The implication is that hard choices have to be made as to the consumer segment to which the offer is to be targeted, and hence the ingredients of that offer. As implied above, the response of most sectors has been to move upmarket so as to follow the affluent 'middle class' consumer in his or her pursuits and aspirations. We strongly suggest that there is a message in this for football and particularly for the design of stadia for the future.

This increased market segmentation, the presumed growth in the importance of leisure and leisure spending for the affluent consumer in the 1990s and the growth in competition for the leisure pound (£) at this time, led the Henley Centre to recommend the formulation of out-of-home leisure activities, not as single events (e.g. 'going to the football match'), but rather as 'integrated leisure experiences, combining the central attraction with a far broader package of associated activities such as eating', a route, it is noted, 'which has long been followed in the USA where sports events are enveloped in a substantial array of activities contributing to a total spectacle' (p. 11).

Finally, such a social realignment of the sport is also recommended by, and has consequences for, postwar changes in local ties of 'community'. Considering the rising levels of mobility and especially with rises in car ownership and the increased reliance on the car for facilitating leisure spending, the Henley Centre found that 'there has been and will continue to be, a gradual erosion of the physical and psychological sense of mobility which once existed' (p. 13).

The implications of all this for top football were threefold: firstly, a close look at the kind of spectator it was trying to attract; secondly, a re-evaluation of the 'benefits' of stadia in difficult-to-access, run-down, inner-city locations – perhaps stadia located closer to motorway networks would now be better; thirdly, perhaps looking beyond those clubs with massive media exposure (in Manchester, Leeds, Liverpool, etc.), the issue of how to sustain the key psychological attachment between clubs and supporters in an age of increasing locational mobility would have to be addressed. As the report stated, 'the question of finding new mechanisms to cultivate this attachment which do not rely on physical proximity is a pressing one' (p. 13). Top football, in short, would need to recognise it was no longer a local working-class sport, but should increasingly target the more affluent, travelling fans.

Reactions to
the League

A debate of two halves

Amidst all the hype and the undoubted successes of 'new' football in England, serious doubts also remain about the nature and longevity of some of the recent changes to the sport. For some commentators inside and outside the sport the 1990s marks nothing less than the beginning of the social and cultural rejuvenation of football in England and the emergence, once again, of the rather Victorian tradition of the English football stadium as an important source of local civic (and commercial) pride, offering up-to-date amenities and facilities, and providing a central community and commercial focus for local business and cultural aspirations.

Rising crowds in the FA Premier League in every season since 1992 show that the new era is popular with spectators. In the Victorian era a new stadium or a new, successful football club helped to put an aspiring town or city on the national map. Today, a new stadium can help revive local interest and set commercial pulses racing, and a top football club can help achieve invaluable European exposure for a supportive city.

At the core of this recent shift in football's fortunes has been the arrival in the sport of a new administrative and entrepreneurial elite which now aggressively 'sells' the sport and its products, especially via TV, to new audiences. This new elite has a late-modern and 'global' view of the sport's marketability and, unlike those men who used to run top clubs, the new order sees profit and the routine tenets of business as integral elements in the practice of sports governance and sports administration. Whereas in the past small businessmen may have 'bought into' their local football club in order to bolster their own civic and business status and perhaps to conduct some trading around materials, building and services on matchdays, today's top football club owners have more diverse commercial links and aspirations. With the arrival of public limited companies in the sport, it is now becoming increasingly difficult to tell who actually owns many of the top English clubs. Some commentators would argue that BSkyB's recent, failed, bid for Manchester United is, nevertheless, the next logical corporate step in the capitalisation and global spread of the influence of the recently successful 'English' commercial football model.

At the same time as this commercial revolution has occurred, recent measured falls in incidents of hooliganism at football grounds in England, for example, have been used to argue for the popular 'rediscovery' of the much-cherished and at least part-mythical traditions of the mutually tolerant and fair-minded English sports crowd. The recent decline of overt racism in English football, the small overtures made by some professional clubs towards 'ethnic minority' support, and the apparent growth in active female support at English football matches have produced a game which now better reflects, so its supporters claim, the variability and tolerance of modern British culture. All-seated stadia have been an important part of this move to a much more 'civilised' climate at top English matches.

Arrests and attendances at Football League matches
(1984/85–1996/97) and FA Premier League and Football
League matches (1992/93–1996/97)

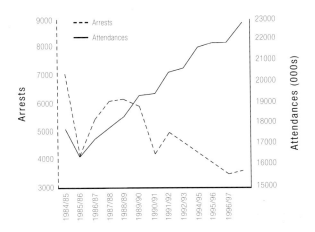

Source: Football Trust *Annual Digest of Football Statistics,* 1996/97

The recent 'mature' and largely orderly response of
fans at Euro '96 in England is also cited as a further sign of
change in these respects and of the international
rehabilitation of the English football public after many
justifiable years as the hooligan pariahs of Europe. In these
accounts the recent hooligan incidents involving followers
of England in Marseilles during France '98 are best read as
the last death throes of a national supporter base which is
itself already in deep transformation. We are ready, in short,
to host World Cup 2006. The new, safer stadia and the
League's promotional glitz has attracted fans – in their
thousands – to watch a vibrant, exciting sport which
exhibits little of the tribal excesses of the 1980s.

Opponents of this strongly 'optimistic' position read the recent period as marking the effective end of the local and 'organic' football crowd. It signals the demise of the self-policing and creative football 'goal end', full of the 'vim and vinegar' in Arthur Hopcraft's famous description of the Spion Kop at Liverpool and characteristic of other great, largely working-class, standing terraces of the 1960s and before. In its wake, critics claim, comes the emergence of the regulated, individuated, surveilled and high-spending, seated, middle-class football audience. From this perspective, stadia at the top level are dull and boring places to be, where crowds – as at Manchester United and Arsenal ('Highbury the library') – have to be urged by officials to offer more vocal support, and where 'safety' rather than excitement or involvement is the order of the day. The 'sounds' of the stadium here are the 'Americanised' public address promotions. Hooliganism also still exists, according to these accounts, it is just that the media 'servants' of top football are now more unwilling to report it – Rupert Murdoch, owner of the satellite football broadcaster, BSkyB, also owns *The Times* and the *Sun* daily newspapers.

To the sceptic, the sorts of people who now, increasingly, make up Premier League football crowds are no more than an ersatz following of promiscuous 'customers', with no real footballing tradition or local ties – save that which is concocted and sold to them by the sport's new marketing gurus. The sport's new entrepreneurs are, themselves, in the sports business only for profit, not for love. Greed rules football and underpins the new Premier League, where the elite no longer cares for the foundations of the sport – the smaller clubs. This is a view of sport as leisure and entertainment rather than as inheritance and authenticity, somewhat akin to the disdain of 'rock' fans for the hyped excesses of 'pop'.

Critics also suggest that new followers at top clubs have no real attachments, born out of the traditional ties of region or place, to their team: they are pointedly customers (not supporters) who choose their clubs, rather than the other way around. In this reading, they have not 'earned' the right to supporter status via the long-term material and psychological deprivation suffered – and welcomed – by the true devotee. These new fans, in short, have it far too easy. Their 'passion' for the sport, if it exists at all, is highly contingent, ultimately transferable and substantially shaped by the new ways in which the sport is mediated and packaged by television. These 'fans' will melt away when the sport eventually sheds – as it surely must – its 'this year's model' vogue.

Top English football has changed over the past decade, of course, but not quite as completely as its supporters might want to suggest or, indeed, as damagingly as its opponents would have it. These highly polarised versions of recent events at least agree that throughout the 1990s, top professional football in Britain, and especially in England, has undergone something of a seismic shift – both in its cultural role and in its economic framing.

Shifting the goalposts

Following the prognosis of the FA *Blueprint*, top English football clubs, led by the new generation of 'professional' administrator/entrepreneurs, have vigorously sought to establish a new and distinctive 'marketised' branding for the sport. Using the key Sky Sports satellite TV channel/FA Premier League relationship as its promotional axis, these top clubs are now aiming at a different fan market. The new League, for example, has very quickly become a major player in leisure markets spanning sport, entertainment, popular culture and television. The clubs which make up the League are also diversifying their activities in ways which open up new leisure markets and which connect them more directly with other local businesses, with important opinion formers (including politicans), and also with national – and increasingly global – commercial concerns.

A number of top English clubs are now owned, not by the local businessmen who were the traditional backbone of the League, but by leisure/media corporations or parent companies which aim to have football as one of a series of businesses or TV-promoted sporting franchises. One international investment company, ENIC, now owns large interests in a number of European clubs, including a 40 per cent share in Glasgow Rangers FC. It is also clear that TV companies and other corporate interests are now very much in the market for purchasing controlling shares in top English football clubs. Twenty British football clubs are now quoted on the Stock Exchange or the Alternative Investors' Market (AIM), in order to aid revenue raising and profit flow – and, in some cases, to realise very large profits for existing shareholders.

Could these football investors and football club owners have predicted that the game in England was going to boom in this way after so many troubled years? Certainly, a number of top executives and owners at football clubs which have become public companies have made enormous profits on their early modest investments. Yet in the late 1980s Martin Edwards, the chief executive at Manchester United, tried to sell his controlling interest in the club for just £10 million. Embarassingly, the potential purchaser, Michael Knighton, could not raise the finances to close the deal. Ten years later United was being valued at something in excess of £600 million, with Edwards' own stake estimated as being worth around £100 million. By contrast, Knighton now owns lowly Carlisle United.

By the early part of 1998 it was also clear that the public flotation of football clubs – hot news to investors just a few months before – had now rather cooled as a potential money spinner for private investors. The Nomura Football Index, which tracks the performance of publicly floated English football clubs, showed that the total value of the football sector had slipped by 20 per cent during the 1997/98 season. By way of comparison, the FTSE index of the 100 top UK companies had risen by 20 per cent in the last three months of the season alone. Analysts attributed the fall in football share prices to the initial hype around football flotations and the unsophisticated internal structures of clubs. Investors had also expected a quicker move to the lucrative pay-per-view TV arrangements, with more top clubs organising their own TV deals.

The financial divide

A 1998 analysis of the English game by the accountants Deloitte and Touche has emphasised the increasing financial gap between larger and smaller clubs in England, and also noted that some larger English clubs were beginning to overtake their continental and world equivalents in terms of annual turnover. Fans of smaller clubs see the extraordinary expenditure by larger clubs on players' salaries and on facilities, and then contrast it with the parlous state of their own club's finances. The Government's Football Task Force, chaired by David Mellor, has recently been looking at the economics of the professional game and is known to be sympathetic to the view that more of the money from the top of the sport should be channelled to struggling Football League clubs. The problem: how could this be achieved when the market was allowed almost free reign in football?

Turnover and operating profit – percentage change 1995/96 to 1996/97 by division

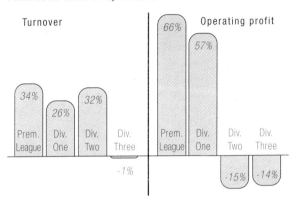

The struggle to make ends meet at the bottom of the Football League
Source: Deloitte and Touche, 1998

The world's richest football clubs

Club	Country	Turnover (£m)
Manchester United	England	87.9
Barcelona	Spain	58.9
Real Madrid	Spain	55.7
Juventus	Italy	53.2
Bayern Munich	Germany	51.6
Milan	Italy	47.5
Borussia Dortmund	Germany	42.2
Newcastle United	England	41.1
Liverpool	England	39.2
Internazionale	Italy	39.1

Top of the world? Some of the top European clubs attract larger crowds than Manchester
United, but none can match the English club's 'external' earnings
Source: Deloitte and Touche, 1998

One possible solution was put forward in April 1998 by the Labour MP for Lincoln, Gillian Merron. She introduced a private member's bill, the Football Sponsorship Levy Bill, which was designed to create an independent levy board with powers to impose levies on football organisations and to allocate football monies 'for the benefit of the game'. She argued:

> The Premiership was founded on greed and as time passes we also see the greed of people who have a passion for making a vast amount of money rather than a passion for football. This is a source of aggravation and despair to fans of Premiership clubs who want to see football flourish and given back to the fans.
> **Reported in the *Guardian*, 8 April 1998**

Without official government backing, the bill had no real chance of success. In any case, the call for a football regulator was hardly likely to be popular with ambitious top clubs or with their investors and shareholders. It did not seem a realistic option for the Task Force itself, whose members included FA Premier League representatives. It might have had support among football fans in a general sense, but fans of top clubs also wanted to see their favourite clubs perform on an even playing surface with the footballing powers of Europe. If top players' wages were held down in England, for example – one way of redirecting funds into the lower reaches of the Football League – how could we compete effectively abroad, or stop our football stars going there for a better pay deal? Of course, when wages were low in England not many of our players went abroad, but it is much easier to work and travel in the new Europe these days.

Clearly, public flotation has not unduly harmed the finances of larger clubs. Some strong football 'brands', for example, Celtic and Manchester United, are still performing very well on the Stock Market – especially during spells when takeover bids involving top media conglomerates have been rumoured. In England, most new football shareholders necessarily look more directly, and dispassionately, at annual company, rather than club or team, performance and results. This has been a hard lesson to learn, as supporters have come to realise that, although better performances on the pitch probably mean larger profits for the parent company, this does not necessarily translate into 'football' decisions being made independently of other considerations. Money for spending on new players, for example, can be refused if the company finances do not look healthy. One example of financial considerations overriding footballing ones occurred when the popular Newcastle United manager, Kevin Keegan, left that club in mid-season because uncertainty about his plans was allegedly threatening the commercial prospects of the club's imminent public flotation.

Under the old Football League regulations, taking profits from football clubs, in the shape of dividends, was strictly limited. No one who went into football could have expected to make huge profits at any time before the 1990s boom. Businessmen went into the sport often for prestige and power and for media coverage, and perhaps to spend some of the cash they had earned elsewhere. This is, increasingly, no longer the case; annual returns on investments can now be very attractive indeed. Writing in relation to the new situation at publicly floated football clubs in England, the *Guardian* sports columnist Richard Williams remarked:

> Their fans [are] unaware of the sole duty of a publicly
> quoted operation which is to deliver the biggest possible

profits to its shareholders. Such a club has not merely the right but the obligation to push its prices – for tickets, replica shirts and broadcasting rights – as high as the market will stand.

Reported in the *Guardian*, 29 April 1996

Football in the community

The more 'traditional' forms of identification with top football clubs in England, typically shaped along the lines of locality, masculinity, class and ethnic exclusivity, are now arguably shifting because of recent changes in the FA Premier League and are increasingly mediated by satellite TV, new patterns of club ownership and control, and by a number of other factors. These include, among other things: ticket price; the centrality of the family audience for the sport; new forms of supporter regulation at matches; and new patterns of consumption around top clubs, reflected in the recent massive sales of club replica kits, licensed leisure goods, etc.

Certainly, the commercial impetuses towards 'flexible accumulation' (the use of stadia as sites for a range of revenue-raising activities of which hosting football matches is just one) which are at the heart of stadium redevelopment and the 'new' football in England, mean that the rather utopian aspirations momentarily voiced in the Taylor Report on the Hillsborough disaster and elsewhere – about possible creative partnerships at local level between clubs, fans and local authorities – are unlikely to materialise at major football clubs in England. 'Democratic' alternatives to the 'commercial' model are available, in a limited sense, at smaller English football clubs – for example, at Bournemouth and at Northampton Town, where supporters' trusts have been set up. They can also be found abroad – at clubs such as St Pauli in Germany

and even at the Spanish giant Barcelona – and there are
clubs which involve supporters in wider aspects of the club's
activities, such as Charlton Athletic, but the 'alternative'
models of control are likely to remain unexplored at larger
football clubs in England.

On a broader level, however, Britain's new centre-left
Labour government, under Tony Blair, has promoted
'employment and educational initiatives' at top football
clubs, including 'classrooms' sited at football stadia, as part
of a scheme to inspire learning in children disaffected by
conventional education. The current Blairite administration
has also identified football as an important political tool and
a key, integrative feature of a modern, regenerated and
'rebranded' Britain. Some football clubs already work
productively with school truants and young offenders as
part of their community programme. Other initiatives have
involved top stars, such as Manchester United's Dwight
Yorke, appearing in computer software programs designed
to aid the teaching of subjects in British schools. In addition
to this, some clubs run their own 'community' initiatives and
'anti-racist' campaigns.

Despite these 'social' aspects of recent changes,
however, the more general economic and structural shifts
in the way top clubs are increasingly being run have not
gone uncontested, and in some places independent
supporter organisations (new fan 'communities') have
emerged to oppose the increasingly 'commercialised'
trajectories of top clubs, or plans to relocate at others
(such as the recent disorderly fan protests at small clubs
like Brighton and Doncaster Rovers; the fan protests
against the club chairmen at both Everton and
Southampton; and the new supporters' groups which
assembled to oppose the Rupert Murdoch ownership bid
at Manchester United). The 'radical' national fan body, the

Football Supporters' Association (FSA), also provides an important and articulate voice for fans in the 1990s and has organised a number of successful supporter campaigns. However, as ownership patterns in the sport have become more complex and more global in scale, the capacity of even organised and resourceful fans to intervene meaningfully in disputes with large clubs at local levels seems relatively limited.

Football
and Television: the New Deal

The new 'marketised' FA Premier League was built squarely on its relationship with television – quite a new departure for British sport. Traditionally, professional football in England had an uneasy relationship with television. Routine overtures from television for coverage of Football League matches, for example, were firmly resisted until the mid-1960s. As late as the mid-1980s the FA was refusing live TV coverage of major foreign matches, in one instance because of a clash with the staging of two Fourth Division games which together attracted just 5,000 hardy spectators. Fifteen years on, live television coverage of football on networked and satellite channels can dominate an entire TV viewing weekend and the amount of general football coverage on television now easily exceeds that of all its competitor sports.

BSkyB and the Premier League

In 1992, the FA and the BSkyB satellite channel announced a new TV deal that would give the Rupert Murdoch-owned channel exclusive live rights to coverage of English football's newly-established FA Premier League. Indeed, the establishment of the new League – very much a triumph of 'the now over history' – was itself predicated on the agreement of a major television deal, inevitably with satellite TV. This new arrangement, which initially (with BBC input) cost £304 million over five years – around six times greater in financial terms than any previous arrangement with TV – seemed to be an 'all-or-nothing' gamble for BSkyB. If the new deal proved to be less than a resounding commercial success, it is difficult to see what else of such potential drawing power satellite television could offer. It would risk being stuck at the margins of broadcasting, caught in a ghetto of cheap and unattractive programming. However, the new relationship with football succeeded as Murdoch's supporters predicted, with Sky Sports channel subscriptions rising steadily and seemingly helping to secure the long-term future of satellite TV in the UK. By 1998, Sky Sports alone had 4.2 million subscribers, most of whom were paying around £24.99 per month for the privilege.

TV money

The size and terms of the new football TV deals provided a ready indication of the key role now played by television in shaping the 'consumption' of English football. The first 'live' football TV deal in England, struck in 1983 and covering five live matches each year for two years, cost a mere £5.2 million. Fifteen years later the new arrangements involved coverage of 60 'live' Premier League matches on satellite at an annual fee to the game which was at least 75 times greater than that paid in 1983. Gate receipts at matches had increased much more slowly during the same period. At some major English clubs today, income raised from sponsorship, advertising, television, hospitality and other sources easily outweighs gate receipts. Although, in overall terms, the money paid in gate receipts by spectators still constitutes the game's largest single income, it is money from sponsorship, merchandising and television which now allows the top English clubs to compete more effectively for players with their main continental rivals.

TV revenues for Football League Division One (1985–1992) and the FA Premier League (1993–2001)

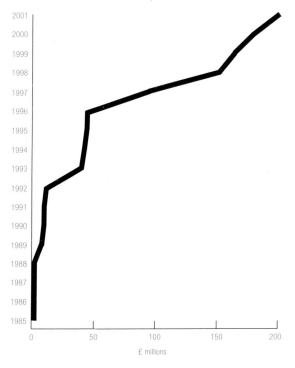

Television: football's new cash cow?
Source: Fletcher Research, 1997

Overcoming consumer resistance among football fans and others to satellite TV was no small task. In the 1980s satellite dishes were unpopular with many people because of their 'downmarket' associations. For some attractive potential customers, 'dishes send out as many signals as they receive. The image of a typical dish owner is an unemployed bloke slumped in front of an ever flickering tube' (the *Guardian*, 14 December 1992). Nevertheless, satellite TV football has clearly been a financial success. Even with the cost of the new improved deal with the FA Premier League from 1997 (£670 million from Sky over five years, plus BBC highlights' cash) which more than doubles the cost of the original agreement, BSkyB's sports' fortunes seemed secure until 2001. BSkyB's income from the Sky Sports channel is now some £1.2 billion per year.

The situation for Football League clubs was not quite so favourable. The Football League was not part of the original link-up with satellite TV. In recent years, satellite has tried to buy up as many of the available top football rights as possible – including Nationwide League coverage. However, while top Premier League clubs could expect to earn around £10 million a year each from the new TV deal, BSkyB's new £125 million five-year deal with the Football League meant that around £20 million a year went to 24 Division One clubs, with just £5 million to be shared by 48 clubs in Divisions Two and Three. This meant around £104,000 a year to ailing bargain basement football clubs. Hardly a king's ransom.

In early 1999 the Office of Fair Trading began examining the relationship between the new league and its major funder, BSkyB, in order to assess whether the latter's exclusive deal for live TV coverage of the FA Premier League restricts competition, as its critics suggest, or provides the best deal at the lowest price for armchair and stadium spectators, as the Premier League claims. Few people would challenge the quality or scale of Sky's coverage; but access to live League TV coverage is now restricted to just one subscription outlet, where monthly fees to customers have risen from as little as the £2.99 special, short-term 'start-up' fee in 1992 to around £24.99 for three Sky Sports channels for satellite subscribers in just six years.

Could individual clubs, as the Office of Fair Trading claims, provide TV football better and cheaper? Would fans, then, see more TV football and would this, in and of itself, be a 'good thing'? Would smaller clubs make more money under different arrangements? Or, does the Office of Fair Trading fail to understand fully the nature and importance of sporting leagues and the difference between sporting competition and the sort of competitiveness which operates in other businesses? Is sport, in short, a special case in terms of business law? Some thought so. As Tony Banks, the Minister for Sport, rather quixotically commented recently in favour of maintaining centralised negotiations: 'Football is a sport which happens to be a business, rather than a business which happens to be a sport'.

Significantly on 1 February 1999 the Italian government adopted a controversial Cabinet decree to limit the rights of any one pay-TV organisation to broadcast Italian Serie A matches live. The decree means that no organisation can own the rights to broadcast 60 per cent of Serie A matches from season 1999/2000. Murdoch's subsidiary company, News Corporation Europe, had been bidding to acquire exclusive rights to Serie A coverage from 1999 to 2005. The decree also proposes that in the event of there being only one bidder for pay-TV rights, any contract signed must last for a maximum of three years. The Italian League planned to protest against the decree, arguing that it actually stifled competition and threatened to damage some clubs (*Financial Times*, 1 February 1999).

Football fans and the new deal

So what of the 'new deal' for those attending matches in England? Part of the Premier League's original case to active supporters, many of whom were strongly opposed to the dismantling of the admittedly outdated Football League and to the selling of TV rights to Sky, was that its new sources of (satellite TV) funding would help keep down ticket prices; TV subscriptions would, in effect, help to subsidise the cost of attending for those who wanted to travel to games. Instead, critics argue, the new League has rapidly ushered in the £1,000 season ticket at some London clubs, with minimum match ticket prices of a staggering £25 and upwards for some 'ordinary' League matches. Ticket prices have been rising annually at some clubs by more than six or seven times the rate of inflation. The total spent by regular supporters at top clubs in the late 1990s could easily top £2,000 – and this is without including the cost of taking children to matches. Rather than keeping ticket prices down, the 'exclusivity' associated with the new Premier League and its new forms of marketing and promotion has seemed to push demand for top football – and match ticket prices – ever upwards, raising claims that a generation of 'traditional' fans of the sport had been effectively excluded from live attendance because of high ticket prices.

The Premier League claims that it is the demand for tickets – and players' wage demands – which inflates ticket prices. Another factor is the comparatively small size of many top English football stadia. In Italy and Spain the stadia at the largest clubs are huge, allowing low prices for the poorest fans and top prices for those who want to be seen in the expensive seats. In most places in England, such a policy is simply not possible. Newcastle United,

Ticket Prices

How far have ticket prices risen since the FA Premier League was established? This is a controversial issue, with some supporters claiming that huge price rises in a matter of a few seasons have resulted in the loss of the lower paid 'traditional' football fan. Perhaps the best way to look at this is to consider the average receipts per spectator before and after the establishment of the new league.

Average receipts per spectator: Football League/ FA Premier League

Year	Average receipts per spectator	% Increase
1986/87	£3.70	–
1988/89	£4.73	28%
1990/91	£6.46	37%
1992/93*	£8.74	35%
1994/95	£10.72	23%
1996/97	£14.60	36%

* The first season of the Premier League.
Source: Football Trust *Annual Digest of Football Statistics*

Prices have been increasing at a pretty stable (and high) rate since at least the mid-1980s. Between 1992 and 1996 average prices for FA Premier League matches increased by 67 per cent. In the same period the national Retail Price Index rose by just 11 per cent. In the period after 1996/97 ticket prices have continued to rise with a number of Premier League clubs charging a minimum match ticket price of £20 and top season tickets costing in excess of £1,000 at some London clubs.

Supporter segmentation by social classification, 1997

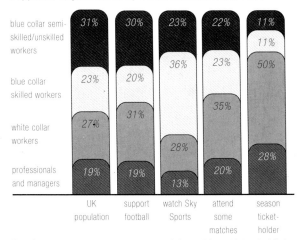

	UK population	support football	watch Sky Sports	attend some matches	season ticket-holder
blue collar semi-skilled/unskilled workers	31%	30%	23%	22%	11% / 11%
blue collar skilled workers	23%	20%	36%	23%	50%
white collar workers	27%	31%	28%	35%	28%
professionals and managers	19%	19%	13%	20%	28%

Those from the lower social classes are the strongest followers of the sport but are least likely to be season ticket holders
Source: Fletcher Research, 1997

for example, has a reported 10,000 waiting list for season tickets for its 36,000-capacity St James' Park, even though local fans still claim that ticket prices are too high. In 1998 most Premier League clubs were playing to an average of over 90 per cent of stadium capacity. It seems clear that stadium capacities in England are now simply too low and ticket prices too high for many who want to attend matches. Will those people currently paying high prices always be happy to attend matches? If not, will the game be able to draw back in those fans who now connect with the sport mainly via TV?

Partly because of cultural shifts, and particularly through the market repositioning of top English football clubs, it seems clear that many younger male fans are also probably being effectively excluded from today's 'live' football audience at the top level. This exclusion comes in two forms – through the mechanism of price and because of their alienation from the new supporter cultures which are being established around the sport. This is perhaps especially so with the emerging dominance of rhetorics about 'safety' and 'safety cultures' concerning spectator behaviour inside football stadia in England.

Here, concern to 'sanitise' and better manage and regulate supporter behaviour has been connected by some oppositional supporter groups to a wider, more cynical, emphasis in the game aimed at further changing the social profile of the active fan base. However, at the same time it must be noted that other previously excluded fans – some females, members of 'minority' groups, more affluent fans – are probably being drawn into the sport because of the cleaner and safer stadia. The implications of these shifts in football crowds away from their strongly working-class traditions are difficult to predict. Did a successful club in the past contribute to social cohesion, for example, when times at work were bad or unemployment came? Can it really have the same impact now?

Footballers and
the Premier League

Having considered the social and cultural impact of the
Premier League, it is now time to ask: what about the
quality of the product? Does the offering on the pitch, the
football itself, measure up to the rising cost of attendance
and the hype off it? What has happened to the condition of
football in England and to the players playing the sport in
the 1990s? Here, too, opinions vary.

Foreign invaders

On the one hand, the Premier League has undoubtedly
drawn in new international stars. At first, these were players
who were coming towards the ends of their long careers –
such as Gullit, Klinsmann and Vialli – who probably came
to England for a lucrative final pay deal and to experience
the special atmosphere and passion associated on the
continent with the sport in this country. Others, such as the
marvellously talented and volcanic sardine poet Eric
Cantona, were exiles from their own countries who had to
go abroad to make a new start.

All of these famous footballing names certainly added
to the allure of the new Premiership competition. Indeed,
during his first, brief, stay in England during the 1994/95
season, Klinsmann and his cavalier colleagues at Tottenham

Hotspur made that club the most popular visiting team in the Premier League. Offering a rather chilling window on the current pervasiveness of football in English culture, a recent survey by the Goethe Institute in London found British school students nominating Klinsmann as the second most famous German, living or dead, behind Adolf Hitler.

Cantona won back-to-back titles in England with two clubs, Leeds United and Manchester United, and he was certainly the catalyst for setting up the latter's dominance of the Premiership throughout the nineties. Cantona was also 'deified' by his many admirers during his stay in England – not least by his central presence in a reinterpretation of Piero della Francesca's painting *Resurrection of Christ* by the Manchester artist Michael Browne. According to the Bishop of Manchester, Cantona's iconic presence in the picture appropriately confirmed the 'absolute hero' status of Christ, Himself. Less auspiciously, Cantona also risked a *sine die* ban from the game in England for fighting with a spectator after being sent off during a match at Crystal Palace. Instead, he completed a long dose of community service, coaching kids in inner city Salford. He was reported to be 'a natural' with disadvantaged youngsters and his experiences later convinced the Government's Football Task Force to recommend the use of work 'in the community' as a means of commuting player suspensions. Can there have been a more influential or controversial player in the entire English game in the 1990s?

As players' salaries in England began to match, and even exceed, those offered abroad, the foreign player trickle to England became a stream and then a flood. In the first season of the Premier League (1992/93), there were 11 foreigners playing in the new League; in season 1998/99, there were 166.

The foreign player invasion 1992–1999

Foreigners playing in the Premiership	
1992/93	11
1993/94	42
1994/95	52
1995/96	66
1996/97	105
1997/98	126
1998/99	166

Source: *Daily Telegraph*, 28 January 1998

In effect, a new more globalised pattern of player mobility has emerged, with the Premier League somewhere near the middle/top of the world hierarchy for its capacity to import top players, and some players in their active prime have recently been recruited to England from France, Holland, Italy, Germany and Spain, as well as from the more usual hunting grounds of Scandinavia and, to a lesser extent, Eastern Europe. Even South Americans have come to England recently – though with rather mixed records of achievement. Foreign football managers have also arrived – Svengalis with the air and background of learned technocrats – and have extolled the virtues of clean lifestyles and 'good' (alcohol-free) diets, as well as, in the case of Ruud Gullit, 'sexy' football. In his first full season in English football, Arsene Wenger won the double of the Premier League and the FA Cup with newly Francophile Arsenal. Luca Vialli is leading something of a renaissance at fashionable and now multinational Chelsea. Here, at a club where racist fans seemed to rule the roost in the 1970s and 1980s, players from all over the globe have helped contribute to the invention of new supporter traditions – and real title hopes –

in south-west London. In 1998 the academic Gerard Houllier, a French Kopite himself while teaching on Merseyside in the 1960s, ended the famous 'boot room' dynasty at Anfield by taking over sole management of Liverpool FC. Ruud Gullit, rejected by Chelsea, now pleads with the 'bar code' army on Tyneside to forget the lost messiah, Kevin Keegan, at Newcastle United plc.

Even in the deeply tribal footballing arguments of Glasgow, the leading managerial protagonists are now foreigners; Dick Advocaat (Rangers) and Dr Joseph Venglos (Celtic) together promise a new era in the Scottish game. As a consequence, a recent Old Firm game in the city offered fewer than a handful of players qualified to represent Scotland. The same is now often true for England when, say, Chelsea play Arsenal. Of the larger English clubs only John Crogory, at Aston Villa, seemed determined to try to succeed at the top level by using only English players.

Can it be that people on 'the island' have finally learned to shelve their local chauvinisms and better accept foreigners as symbolic representatives of their communities via their revered place in the local football club? Certainly the new freedom of movement offered to professional players from the European Union by the historic legal case brought by the Belgian player, Jean-Marc Bosman, has speeded up player transfers around the world. At the end of their contracts, players can now move with no transfer fee payable – just like any other EU worker. Players are therefore much more powerful now and better able to shape their own destinies. British players, however, are still among the most reluctant to travel abroad – where language and cultural barriers remain daunting prospects for most. Ian Rush, the Welsh international forward, remarked memorably that the worst thing about his miserable time playing in Italy in 1987/88 was that, 'It was like being in a foreign country'. He soon returned to score more goals in England. Things have changed now, but Rush has been followed to the daunting Serie A in Italy by no more than a handful of British players.

Players' Transfers and the Bosman Ruling

From the early days of the sport, every professional footballer had to be registered with the FA and the Football League. If players moved clubs, their registration had to be transferred between clubs and was subject to the approval of the FA and the Football League. Usually the selling club would demand a fee for the transfer of registration (a transfer fee). Restrictions were first placed on the mobility of players from 1891. From that date up until 1963, players who wanted to move clubs had to make a transfer request to their club. If their own club refused the request, the player was effectively tied as long as the club was willing to offer to retain players on the same minimum conditions and wages as they currently enjoyed. The system was designed to limit wages and to prevent all the top players finishing up at the richest clubs.

In 1963 the Eastham case in the High Court found the retain-and-transfer system to be 'an unreasonable restraint of trade'. From this point, if clubs failed to exercise their option to re-hire players on a further contract of at least similar length, players could leave the club with no transfer fee payable.

From 1977/78 real 'freedom of contract' arrived. This meant that at the end of their contracts, players could exercise their option to leave the club if they so wished. If a player's own club had offered them new terms which were at least as attractive as the old ones, then the selling club was entitled to a transfer fee. If clubs could not agree a fee, it was decided by an independent tribunal. When under contract, players or their agents were not allowed to initiate transfer moves; it was up to the potential buying club to approach the holding club.

This system lasted until the ruling by the European Court of Justice on 20 September 1995 in the case of the Belgian professional footballer Jean-Marc Bosman. This EU ruling established the free movement of EU players, once their contracts have ended, between clubs from different EU countries with no fee payable. Some countries have adopted the same principles for transfers within EU countries. Others have abolished transfer fees for players who are over 24 years of age and out of contract. This is to ensure incentives for clubs to continue to raise their own young players.

Thus far, Liverpool's Steve McManaman is the most celebrated post-Bosman case. His club tried to sell him, against his will, to Barcelona more than one year before his contract expired. The club feared the loss of a potential £12 million transfer fee if McManaman was allowed to see out his Liverpool contract. The player joined Real Madrid in 1999 for no transfer fee, but for wages reputed to be around £60,000 per week.

Historians will point out that Scottish professionals playing south of the border have, for more than a century, punctured the notion that professional footballers in this country have always been strongly locally drawn. It is also true that at some of the largest clubs in England today – Liverpool and Manchester United, for example – locally produced players still vie very strongly for selection with expensive foreign imports. In fact, Liverpool in the late 1990s has many more local products in its first team squad than ever played for the club during their overwhelmingly successful years of the 1970s and 1980s, when Scottish and Irish 'imports' were dominant.

Nevertheless, there are many complaints about the number of foreign players in the English game. These have come most strongly from the Professional

Footballers' Association – the players' union in England.
The union's concern has been the alleged arrival of many
'ordinary' but cheap foreign imports to the Premier
League to take the place of 'ordinary' domestic players,
who may in the past have come through the breeding
grounds of lower league football. As players' wages and
transfer fees for contracted players have continued to rise
in England, hard-pressed managers on small budgets in
the Premier League and in Division One of the Football
League have gone abroad in search of technically
superior, if limited, foreign recruits. The Bosman ruling and
the growth of Football Academies at the top level have
further contributed to the plight of smaller clubs in
England which, in the past, might have hoped to raise
much-needed income from producing and selling on
young players to larger English clubs. In 1996/97, net
income from transfers for clubs in the lowest division in
the Football League was around £2 million – more or less,
the same figure as was recorded in 1990/91. Over the
same period total transfer spending by English clubs on
domestic and foreign purchases had increased by more
than £150 million on a direct comparison. Most of the
increased spending on transfers involved deals between
FA Premier League clubs and more especially on deals
done with foreign clubs. Before the 1997/98 campaign,
pre-season transfers by English clubs involving foreign
players alone exceeded £100 million – more than double
the total football transfer spending in England in 1990/91.

Developing young players

What has happened to counter the invading foreign football
hordes? The new Football Academies, introduced under
the auspices of the Football Association's *Charter for*

Football in 1998 and sited at 34 licensed top professional clubs, are intended to assist in giving top clubs many more opportunities to work for longer with local younger players' while at the same time requiring the clubs to safeguard the educational side of a youngster's development. These, coupled with Centres of Excellence at clubs, will now allow them much more contact with good local prospects from eight years of age right up to the point of signing professional contracts. The new structures are to adopt the continental Ajax model of using small-sided games for very young players. The aim is to limit the number of competitive matches played by youngsters and to bring English clubs up to the same standard of training that foreign clubs have been giving their own young players.

The traditionally harsh coaching regimes at English professional clubs and the strengths and tradition of the English Schools FA had usually meant top clubs in England had been extremely limited in the time they were allowed per week to coach youngsters and in the ages of children they were allowed to work with. Once inside a club, a youngster who was 'too interested' in college might soon be branded as 'lacking focus' on the (limited) prospects of becoming a pro. The new 'enlightened' club coaching regimes allow for tuition and homework time to take care of educational needs. It also allows time for intensive coaching work when players are likely to benefit from it most – when they are young. Under these rules, the youngsters who don't make it – the majority – will still have a decent chance of a different career.

At very young ages, as we have said, there is no competitive eleven-a-side football allowed – just seven-a-side football. Dave Richardson, the Premier League's Director of Youth Coaching, sees coaching, rather than playing, as the way ahead now for young players. He argues:

> We are still a games-oriented nation. Even now, at
> professional level, you hear people saying they would
> much rather play than coach. No wonder, because it is
> much less work. Anyone can run a team and hand out
> the shirts, but to coach you have to use your head, and it
> takes planning.

Dario Gradi, the respected coach at Crewe Alexandra,
another Academy club, agrees with these sentiments.
He even objects to the Academy Leagues set up for
under-17 and under-19 club teams because: 'The only
purpose of youth football is to try to produce some skilful
players, and I don't think there should be any emphasis
on winning the league' (reported in the *Daily Telegraph*,
21 December 1998).

Will all of this new, more 'scientific' work with
youngsters result in producing better and more local
contenders at the very highest levels? Will it also improve
the general quality of English footballers, producing more
rounded and more mature individuals? It is too early to say,
as yet. However, the economics of this new approach are
also interesting. The new Liverpool FC Academy, boasting
14 pitches, an indoor hall, a medical centre and four
classrooms, has cost the club a reported £13 million to
build. Most clubs would balk at that kind of price – and the
minimum costs of setting up an academy under the new
FA Charter means that smaller professional clubs will find it
very difficult to invest in this way. (However, one smaller
club, Peterborough United, has invested £500,000 in its
own Academy and already has top clubs preparing to bid
millions for its local youth products.) Even at Liverpool, to
find just one Michael Owen or Robbie Fowler through such
initiatives might mean that the building costs of an
Academy even of this scale are effectively covered. Or at

least that would have been the case in a pre-Bosman football world, when a top player moving on would guarantee a large transfer fee.

The 'prune effect'

As the effects of Bosman become more apparent and transfer fees disappear for players out of contract, it is possible that the situation for smaller English clubs may worsen. Given the level of wages in the Premier League, it is harder now for Football League clubs to buy young Premier League reserves and prepare them for lucrative re-sale after 'improvement' work. Players may now spend virtually their whole careers in reserve team football, 'unable' to afford to move to other clubs. Able players at lower levels are likely to resist lengthy contracts in the hope of securing better deals at larger clubs (though this, itself, will become a case of careful assessment). In any case, smaller clubs may not be able to afford long contracts.

The total amount of money spent on deals, as players move, will probably keep on increasing. The money which used to circulate 'in the game' – and which might even have been used to buy new stands or other facilities – will now be more likely to find its way into the pockets of players and their growing band of advisors. This is happening already at the top level, where £2 million annual deals, plus signing on fees, are no longer unusual for the very best players. In 1996/97 the average player wage in the FA Premier League was just short of £210,000 – it will be rather higher now. In the same season, the average Third Division wage – for a playing career averaging about eight years – was around £28,000. One suspects the figure will have risen rather less quickly since then.

The booming Premiership

Clubs' turnover

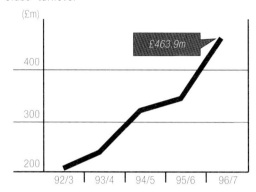

Players' earnings

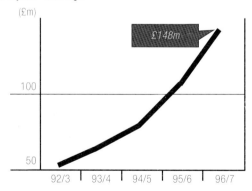

Total turnover increases dramatically – but so do the players' wages
Source: Deloitte and Touche, 1998

Alan Sugar, the chief executive at Tottenham Hotspur, calls this recent trend of transfer money being converted into player wages the 'prune effect' – big money comes into the game (from TV and sponsors) and rapidly moves through and out of it again into the pockets of top players and agents. The players can justifiably point out that they are responsible for the product – the game – that ultimately makes all the cash, so what is wrong with them reaping the 'proper' market rewards for their abilities? In a hard business such as football, and in the current buyer's climate, few players will draw compliments or even thanks anyway for 'rewarding' their seller clubs by signing a short contract extension in return for a transfer involving a compensatory fee from the buying club. Indeed, at the very moment that clubs are trying to get their own valuable assets to agree contracts in order to guarantee them a seller's fee, they are often also snapping up players from a rival club with no fee involved. In football, it seems, there is no honour among thieves.

The new player image

The new player mobility paths and the Academy approach of the 1990s means that few top English clubs are now looking to Scotland for top quality youngsters or proven players. The Scots, who once helped English top clubs dominate in Europe, now seem some way off the top international pace. These days, continental players, particularly from France, Holland and Scandinavia, offer both the physical and technical qualities necessary to succeed in the British game. They also offer the sorts of lifestyles and the personal 'maturity' increasingly demanded by coaches and sponsors in top sport. The new breed of foreign coach working in Britain knows, for example, that with foreign playing recruits he is probably rather less likely to be faced with potentially embarrassing tabloid coverage about his new star's 'late nights out with all the trimmings'. (Though he may end up with frustrating cases of player 'stress' or 'stay-away' tantrums if new deals don't work out.) Top players' agents and sponsors are no longer simply selling their clients' ability on the pitch, they are also selling their capacity to market products from shampoo (Ginola, McAteer) to mobile phones (Wright) to clothes (David James, Giggs) and even places (Jamie Redknapp's 'Bournemouth is nice' ads); having the right image is therefore crucial. Top players in England are rather more likely now to be lauded locally by their supporters and financial backers, not because they have gently acceded to fans' demands that they 'come out for a few pints', but because they appear in news coverage revealing their newly-found interest in a 'quiet night in', perhaps for a spot of meditation and self-reflection, or even – in the case of Arsenal captain Tony Adams – a little poetry reading. As the 'medicalisation' of everyday life proceeds apace and as the occupational culture of top players in England becomes more publicity-conscious, more cosmopolitan and technocratic, and less class-bound – more middle-class parents now seem to favour the sport as an 'acceptable' occupation for clever sons – so the language of addiction has increasingly replaced that of cultural inclusion when describing top players who continue to insist on being 'just one of the lads, out for a bevvy'.

Players such as the hyper-active Paul Gascoigne and the snarling Vinnie Jones now seem increasingly anachronistic – immutable products of 1980s English football. The confessional and prodigal virtues of the 1990s are exemplified by Paul Merson, an English player who recently, and lucratively, left top club Middlesbrough because of its alleged drinking culture. The 1990s is also an era of lower middle-class level-headedness; of the clean cut and remarkable Michael Owen, for example, every mother's son, or daughter's preferred boyfriend. These are players whose earning potential has rocketed footballers belatedly into the highest echelons of the list of top sporting earners around the world.

Just as 'ordinary' top tennis players have become affluent (if sometimes rather dull) athletes rather than personalities in the 1990s, so too could English footballers of the new period. Other types of player – the perplexing Stan Collymore, for example – who are neither 'lads', nor are apparently able to cope with the new mental demands of being a top performer, might end up, tellingly and rather embarrassingly, in psychological counselling. With these important shifts in approach in mind, it is hard to avoid the conclusion that the new era of Premier League hype and massive player salaries has produced quite a different perspective, both inside clubs and in the stands, on the lifestyles and identities of players and on footballing links with the continent. This integration of the English and European game may have important implications for our view of ourselves as 'Europeans' beyond the narrow confines of sport.

Club versus Country

Arguably, the general quality of top club football played in the Premier League in England – and even in Scotland – over the past few years has improved because of the changes outlined above. However, this does not mean that these recent changes have all been positive for English or for Scottish football. In European club competitions in the 1990s, even with foreign players now on board, the record of English club sides has been rather poor, and the record of Scottish clubs has been even worse. Since their dominance of the competition in the late 1970s and early 1980s, and until Manchester United's European Cup run in 1999, no English club has reached the Final of the Champions Cup competition; not since the fateful evening back in May 1985 when 39 mainly Italian fans lost their lives following hooliganism and a wall collapse at the Juventus v. Liverpool European Cup Final in Brussels. This disaster, broadcast live across Europe, resulted in a five-year ban for English clubs from European club competitions and crystallised the English reputation for spectator thuggery and xenophobia.

Many coaches in England feel that the game is still suffering the ill effects of this forced exclusion from top international competition. The recent playing record in European club competitions suggests they may be right.

Even Manchester United, reputedly the most valuable football club – perhaps the most valuable sports club – in the world and the dominant force in the English game in the 1990s, had to wait more than thirty years to add to its solitary European Cup win. Only in the weak and now defunct European Cup Winners' Cup competition have English clubs achieved some regular recent success – a fact which perhaps reveals more than anything the English penchant for domestic Cup football in the face of widespread European indifference to this sort of knockout event. This obvious lack of international club success has brought charges that the Premier League is over-hyped – long on excitement and the sort of competitiveness traditionally demanded by the English football crowd, but short on real quality and technique. This has led to the re-examination of long-standing debates about the virtues and weaknesses of the British game.

The new era should have brought with it a more cerebral and more considered approach to the English game, it has been argued. In turn, this should have produced more success in international football, where games tend to take on a more chess-like quality, as British players try to come to terms with the sudden acceleration and better techniques of foreign players and with the challenges posed, for example, by climate. Winning international tournaments in high summer these days is often down to good decision-making, skill and stealth rather than to the traditional British virtues of high tempo football, team spirit and strength.

The need for technical excellence is even more the case today, because improved training methods abroad have provided for more of the physical and mental strength which the British used to consider to be to their own exclusive advantage – especially when facing foreign opposition on home soil. For example, during the European Championships of 1992 the then England coach, Graham Taylor, complained that the home nation (Sweden) had succeeded in beating the English because 'They played the English style better than we did'. In other words, the Swedes – powerful, athletic and skilful, if lacking in real imagination – simply wore down a technically limited, methodical and dull England side.

Seven years on from Sweden, and with the potential benefits of a new 'internationalised' Premier League, has much really changed for the England national team? In the World Cup Finals in France in 1998, England were eliminated in heroic circumstances by Argentina, in a dramatic penalty shootout. However, they still only managed to defeat the demoralised Colombians and the weak and soon-eliminated Tunisians.

In England, as in Spain – but not, for example, in Holland – it may be that club football is simply much more important to fans than the national team. Spain's international results in tournaments have been as disappointing as our own over the past two decades. Certainly, the historic rivalry between the amateur patricians at the Football Association who run the national team in England and the professional businessmen, managers and players who have traditionally run the professional clubs here is one which is inscribed deeply in the sport's history. Perhaps it is indicative of the general world view of the Football Association that it has never seen it necessary to add the prefix 'English' to its title; it has always been the FA, the first national football association – and for a long time one largely indifferent to the interests of professional clubs or to that of the development of the sport beyond these shores. Not until 1950 did England first agree to compete in the World Cup, and then only to suffer international humiliation at the hands of the little-considered USA. It may also be indicative of future trends that the fans of one of England's 'national' clubs, Manchester United, recently started chanting 'Argentina' at matches and made unpleasant suggestions about where the England team might best be put, apparently in support of their hero David Beckham, who had been taunted by rival fans in England because of his World Cup sending-off against the South Americans. The real message here may be that it is the Premier League's Manchester United, rather than England, which is increasingly seen by their fans as the footballing world power.

The struggles between the interests of the top professional clubs in this country and those of the wider footballing community – including the national team – continue to rumble on today, despite the fact that the new Premier League is actually run under the auspices of the Football Association itself. It is, after all, the FA Premier League, and it is quite distinctive in this sense from the clubs it left behind, under the control of the Football League, following the 'great divide' in 1992. However, the Premier League is in reality run by its own Executive under the close supervision and direction of the 20 Premier League chairmen. The FA intervenes on matters of discipline and has recently appointed a 'sleaze-buster' to monitor the financial propriety of clubs. But, who really takes much notice? In fact, in the worldwide power struggles between the national associations and the professional clubs, the latter seem increasingly to hold the whip hand. This fact was revealed most starkly when, towards the end of 1998, an independent commercial organisation, *Media Partners* – which had previously advised European football on TV deals – emerged with plans to run an alternative European club competition, funded by television. This privatised version of European club football would ensure that a much higher proportion of the income made from the European game returned to the clubs. Unsurprisingly, the most powerful clubs welcomed this intervention and used it to 'encourage' UEFA to revamp its club competitions in ways which offered more play for clubs from the top footballing nations and also much more money for the top clubs. This having been conceded by an embattled UEFA, for the moment *Media Partners* have disappeared off the public stage – but don't be surprised to see them (or others like them) back in the international football bidding stakes soon.

Arsene Wenger, manager at Arsenal, recently questioned, for example, whether football fans in England were actually that interested in World Cup qualifying matches which matched top nations against international minnows. Wouldn't north London football fans prefer to watch Arsenal or Spurs, he asked, rather than losing yet another weekend of top Premier League action simply to watch a poor England stumble against little Moldova or Georgia? It is a good question and one worth considering for a while.

This was not the first time in recent years that the attractions of top club football had been favourably compared with those offered by international teams. In the early 1990s Silvio Berlusconi, the owner of the then all-conquering AC Milan (a team built around outstanding Dutch players), had claimed that national team football would decline in popularity as the top European clubs became ever stronger. The wealth of top clubs in Europe now meant they could assemble some of the world's top players in teams which would be more than a match for most national sides. This seemed like a compelling argument. However, as football has globalised in terms of the mobility of players and access via TV to coverage of top players all around the world, it has also exhibited localising effects as fans continue to celebrate the ties that give them some rooted national affiliations through sport. Perhaps this is especially the case for the post-Soviet and Eastern bloc emerging 'new' nations, where national and ethnic pride is being given full reign for the first time in many years.

The World Cup remains the largest media sports event in town, as shown by France '98, and there seems little or no diminution in public interest. In fact, as part of an emerging power play between the clubs and national team competition, Sepp Blatter, the new FIFA president, recently suggested the idea of staging a World Cup every two years rather than on the four-yearly cycle which has always been favoured. At first sight, this is an attractive proposition. The finals are profitable and popular. TV and sponsors are waiting for the opportunity to support a two-yearly competition. The move would also strengthen FIFA's international position. Yet there are also numerous objections – although FIFA has difficulty recognising them. They include: striking the best balance between club and national team football; the increasing amount of football that top players now play; the claims for fixture space of the various confederation international championships, in Europe, Asia, South America and Africa; and finally, the 'scarcity' factor – which means that the international TV audience still looks forward to seeing all the world's great national teams play in one competition every four years.

Perhaps the major stories of the 1998 World Cup Finals concerned the sense of common national identity, across ethnic and racial barriers. This was promoted by the success of the multiracial French team in winning the World Cup for the first time, and further through the great pride invested by the people of Croatia in their war-torn nation's achievement in finishing in a very honourable third place. Of course, the Finals are also an important market-place these days for players' sponsors and agents to maximise client exposure and make a case for negotiating new deals or transfers with clubs, as well as for national leagues to better promote their international case for being the elite league in the world game.

The FA Premier League, for example, has made much of the presence in the 1998 winning French squad of Leboeuf, Desailly, Vieira and Petit, all players who had chosen to play their club football in England in 1998/99 (although, most of the successful French team actually play abroad elsewhere in Europe – the outstanding winning trio of Thuram, Deschamps and Zidane, for example, all play in Serie A, in Italy). In this scenario, the defeated Brazilians 'represented' the leagues of Spain and Italy. Despite its claims to the contrary, most knowledgeable observers of the game still put the money-rich FA Premier League behind the Italian League – and possibly the Spanish League – in terms of the European hierarchy of top leagues. There is a case to even consider the claims of the ransacked French League to match the FA Premier League for the quality of its football. Certainly, in recent European club competitions, French clubs have often done more than hold their own against the 'cream' of the English club game (e.g. Manchester United v. Monaco; Liverpool v. Paris, St Germain and Strasbourg; Arsenal v. Lens, etc.)

For some fans, far from losing interest in the England national football team, the glamour and the hype of the Premier League has helped to fuel media-orchestrated national interest around the England squad, and especially around the fate of the team manager. This attention seems to have grown ever more burdensome with the passing years. Glenn Hoddle is simply the latest, if the most bizarre, victim of this media pressure-cooker. The pitfalls facing each new England manager and his hapless squad seem to have been read by the press as a tale of nothing less than the failing state of the English nation itself.

Not far below the surface in these media accounts is often an implicit racism or imperialism which charts how far the nation has fallen from previous grace as measured by football defeats suffered at the hands of nations who can barely be considered our 'civilised' equals, never mind our footballing betters. Such attitudes may also be found among the army of violent supporting recruits who still find satisfaction in mirthlessly trashing foreign towns to remind the locals that once the English really did rule by brute hand and force of will – and at much more than football.

The existence of the FA Premier League seems to have done little thus far to disrupt this prevailing pattern of international failure and violent fan retribution. Far from providing the more sophisticated context from which English players – and fans – might transfer their abilities to an international stage, it is now alleged that younger English players are getting far too few opportunities to show what they can do at the highest levels, as foreign stars – and many imported journeymen – clog up the arteries of the English club game. In Scotland some attempts have been made to address this problem by the introduction of a ruling that all Scottish clubs must include some Scottish players under 21 years of age among their substitutes for first team matches. In England no such step has yet been recommended or taken by the Premier League.

Managing Top Clubs

Managing a top club these days has become an extraordinary and skilful balancing act. The success of the Premier League itself has added considerably to the burden. Judgement is everything here. To sign a top young player on a contract for less than four or five years these days makes little sense; any shorter, and one soon starts to wonder about losing his services to a rich predator for no reward.

Signing foreign players may raise other questions about suitability and adaptability. At current wages a long contract for a top star could also cost as much as £8 million – a costly mistake if things don't work out, especially if your prize asset becomes unwanted and perhaps unsellable, say, within a year. Managers need large, experienced playing squads, but they also need to be able to offer opportunities to eager and talented youngsters. They must keep all squad members happy – but also keep consistency and continuity in the team. They must ensure, come what may, that their talented non-EU players play 75 per cent of matches in order that they can renew their work permits – though the British Government has been reviewing the work permit issue for non-EU players. They must, in short, do everything.

New managers need to plan for the future, in the full knowledge that anything they put in place now, but which is aimed for the longer term, will be a waste of time and effort if first team results in the first six months of their arrival are not up to scratch. Concentrating on the longer-term foundations of a club and on unravelling the mess left by the previous manager, can help save the club, but it can also lose you your job even before it has really begun. What happens in a single week can feel like almost *everything* at a club working on a 'results' tightrope at the highest level.

Above all else, managers must keep their clubs in the FA Premier League. The new economics of football at the highest levels now mean that the bare financial costs of relegation from the FA Premier League these days probably starts at around £10 million and rises for most clubs. But there is much more at stake here than mere income. Loss of status and morale brought by relegation is also a huge blow. Relegation with a raft of players on lengthy contracts at Premier League pricing levels is also to court possible financial ruin. Relegation means the value of your saleable assets is likely to nosedive as potential bidders come, smelling desperation.

Of the current managers in the Premier League only Alex Ferguson has had a decent stay at his current club. But even Ferguson was, reportedly, one bad result from the sack earlier in his Old Trafford career. He would probably not be afforded the same grace today. Now, apart from possibly Arsene Wenger, Ferguson is probably the only serving manager in the Premier League who is reasonably secure in his post. New arrivals here are inherently expendable. Even 'middle-term' managers these days are only a few bad results away from the consequences of pressure and anxiety from supporters, a tabloid 'spin', and then consideration for the sack. The administrations of all medium-sized and smaller clubs at the top level are quite paralysed by the fear of possible relegation, so dark and deep is the chasm which now divides the FA Premier

League from the Football League. To act hastily is to invite possible free fall into oblivion. Not to act at all might mean slow death. This has produced the ludicrous situation of some English managers now being sacked in September and October after merely a handful of games – although none have yet suffered the fate of Real Madrid's Jupp Heynkes, who was sacked for domestic failings just days after the club had actually won the European Cup in 1998. The sum total of all of this is that fear of failure largely rules administrations from midway and towards the bottom of the FA Premier League. Too afraid to act, too frightened to fail; this is an increasingly difficult place to work.

Some Final Comments

So, in summary, what has happened to top football in this country since the FA Premier League came into being? It is a complicated story. The game has certainly dragged itself out of the terrible hole in which it was almost buried in the 1980s. Hooligan-haunted and lacking in expertise and real leadership, and sited in outmoded stadia, football seemed an unlikely candidate to become a popular and pacified spectator sport in the 1990s.

The government and public reaction to the Hillsborough disaster, and satellite TV's need to attract more viewers in the early 1990s, provided the cash to launch the new FA Premier League, which has since gone from strength to strength commercially and in terms of its cultural centrality. Football now seeps into almost every aspect of popular culture and sometimes seems to constitute a new civic realm. When the England football team manager expresses an opinion on almost any subject, we tend to expect a response from the Prime Minister or from one of his Cabinet. Clearly, football is also very much part of the political agenda.

In football's darker days no politician was willing to stand up and proclaim him/herself a football fan. Today, virtually every notable public figure wants their football allegiance properly advertised. If they have none, one will soon be invented by a helpful spin doctor. Football is hot and it is rich. But not everybody in football is either hot or rich. Most of the 92 League clubs in this country still make an annual loss. Very small clubs continue to walk the tightrope of disastrous finances set against the distant hope of better results, potentially larger gates and the prospects of selling a young star. Each of these is less likely, however, now the Premier League is with us. New legislation on transfers, the glut of foreign imports and the arrival of Football Academies is likely to make life even harder at the lower levels. No smaller club's future is secure today. But then, no smaller club's future was ever really secure, it seems.

Television is much more powerful in football today. The rhythms of top football in England no longer hum to the universal call of 3 p.m. on Saturday afternoons. Followers of top clubs must now attune their support to Sunday, Monday, even Thursday appointments, in order to satisfy TV schedules. FA Cup weekends are just that, with fixtures spread over the entire period and the next round draw often taking place – for the benefit of TV – before all matches from the previous round have even been played. BSkyB has even managed to alter the Premier League fixture list in order to try to guarantee a seasonal climax – why 'waste' the top matches at the start of the season? However, Sky Sports has been a remarkable promotional tool for the FA Premier League. Being a dedicated sports channel, it has also offered serious 'magazine' coverage for the sport of a kind that was never possible for terrestrial TV companies. Nor do the latter have the cash to compete in football's TV bidding wars.

On the finance and control side of football, the future of many of the top clubs is no longer simply in the hands of those who direct the 'football' side of the business. Parent companies, shareholders, the vagaries of the market and future corporate interests are all a long way from the 'stressed concrete and meat market millionaires' who used to watch over the future of top clubs. The single funders which remain now often 'watch' their playthings from some off-shore tax haven. The sense that local capital is involved in some identifiable way in shaping the future of many of the biggest football clubs in England has now become something of a romantic fiction. Fans can still protest against those who seem to control their clubs – but it will become increasingly hard to know exactly where, and how, to apply popular pressure for change. In the future the question of whether money is available to improve the side will depend less on the prospects of championships, promotion and relegation than it will on the timing of reports to shareholders and the state of company business elsewhere. Top clubs continue some social duties, but really they relate to fans now mainly via what supporters – their customers – buy.

On the playing side, the new finances of football have also had their effects. Results are becoming more predictable, for example, founded as they increasingly are on the wage bills of top clubs. Finishing positions in the FA Premier League now largely reflect who is paying what and to whom. High payers finish first; low salary bills usually mean relegation. The 'double' of the League Championship and FA Cup, so difficult to achieve in the first hundred years of the Football League, is now commonplace as the strong become ever stronger – witness Manchester United's (the richest club in the world) recent and historic treble. The idea that a 'normal', provincial club might battle to win the title – as Nottingham Forest did in the late 1970s, not 'buying' the title as Blackburn Rovers were impressive in doing in the 1990s – seems almost laughable today. The richest clubs buy the best players, who are freer, and more willing, to move today to clubs offering the highest salaries. At the highest level, player loyalty to a single club seems like an idea whose time has well and truly gone – unless, of course, players are already lodged at the biggest and most successful clubs.

The arrival of foreign stars has added glamour and some quality to the Premier League, but there remain nagging doubts about the real strength of the English club game. Despite recent improvements, the record of English clubs in Europe since 1992 is really quite poor. There is also growing concern about the effects of foreign imports on young local players. Will the latter get a chance to develop? How will the national team fare if top stars from abroad continue to fill club team sheets? The threat posed by the growth in European club competitions to the English game is surely another sign of the times. The expanding Champions League will pressure domestic leagues. Today, top managers, like Alex Ferguson, say only that their ultimate priority is the Champions League. But we may not be too far from the day when top English clubs will, in effect, have two first team squads – one for weekend domestic work; another for the weekly European League challenges. Television and the necessary capital is there now to secure a European League. Will this mean smaller English clubs perhaps becoming 'nurseries' for their richer neighbours to give out-of-favour squad players a chance to play? This already happens on the continent, where the history and traditions of smaller clubs are perhaps guarded a little less feverishly than they are in England. It seems unlikely, like it or not, that we will have to wait too long for the arrival of a European League. How this will help further reshape domestic football remains, as they say, to be seen.

Further Reading

Brown, A (ed.). *Fanatics*, London, Routledge, 1998.

Conn, D. *The Football Business*, Edinburgh, Mainstream, 1997.

Fletcher Research. *Net Profits: How to Make Money Out of Football*, London, Fletcher Research, 1997.

Fynn, A. and Guest, L. *Out of Time: Why Football isn't Working*, London, Simon and Schuster, 1994.

Horton, E. *Moving the Goalposts*, Edinburgh, Mainstream, 1997.

King, A. *The End of the Terraces*, London, Leicester University Press, 1998.

Kuper, S. *Football Against the Enemy*, London, Orion, 1994.

Redhead, S. *The Passion and the Fashion*, Aldershot, Avebury, 1993.

Russell, D. *Football and the English*, Preston, Carnegie Publishing, 1997.

Sugden, J. and Tomlinson, A. *Who Rules the People's Game: FIFA and the Contest for World Football*, Cambridge, Polity Press, 1998.

Williams J. and Wagg, S (eds.). *British Football and Social Change*, Leicester, Leicester University Press, 1991.